WORLD CRISIS: ROBERT KURZ'S ANNOTATED INTERVIEW

CHARLES ODEVAN XAVIER

**Create Space Independent Publishing Platform
New Charleston, SC (USA) - 2017**

Charles Odevan Xavier, 2017 - All rights reserved

To the members of the Radical Critical Group [Grupo Crítica Radical] of the capital of Ceará - A group that proposes, from the Categorical Critique to the immanent categories of the society producing merchandise, a new sociability no longer mediated by money and merchandise.

- INTRODUCTION ....
- KARL MARX: LIVE OR CORPSE? ....
- THE QUESTION OF CREDIT AND INTEREST ....
- MONEY VERSUS DOLLAR ....
- THE CONTRADICTION THAT EXPLAINS THE CRISIS ....
- THE STATE AS LAST CREDITOR ....
- THE STATE: AGAIN THE SAVIOR? ....
- OF THE VALUE FOR THE FUNCTIONAL RELATIONSHIP ....
- THE QUESTION OF THE LABOR ......
- CAPITALISM REDUCED TO ITS REAL VALUATION CONDITIONS ....
- THE TENSION IN THE ADMINISTRATION OF THE CRISIS ....
- THE DISTINCTION BETWEEN "PRODUCTIVE WORK" AND "IMPRODUCTIVE WORK" ....
- AN IMPROPER OCCUPATION ...
- THE ABSTRACT WORK SYSTEM LEADS TO THE ABSURD AT YOUR OWN ....
- AND LEFT? ....
- THE LEFT AND THE SUBJECT-OBJECT DIALECTICS OF MODERN FETISHISM ....

VIRTUAL CAPITALISM ....

CAPITALIST DESTRUCTION OF NATURE ....

POST-MODERN THOUGHT AND NEOLIBERALISM ....

PARADOXAL SUBJECTS ....

RENEWAL OF POLICY .....

SOLIDARY ECONOMY AS PLACEBO ....

EXPLANATORY NOTES ....

THE STATE: AGAIN THE SAVIOR? 22

OF THE VALUE FOR THE FUNCTIONAL RELATIONSHIP 24

THE QUESTION OF THE LABOR 24

CAPITALISM REDUCED TO ITS REAL CONDITIONS OF VALORIZATION 25

THE TENSION IN THE ADMINISTRATION OF THE CRISIS 26

THE DISTINCTION BETWEEN "PRODUCTIVE WORK" AND "IMPRODUCTIVE WORK" 27

AN IMPROPER OCCUPATION 28

THE ABSTRACT WORK SYSTEM LEADS TO THE ABSURD TO SELF 29

VIRTUAL CAPITALISM 32

CAPITALIST DESTRUCTION OF NATURE 34

POST-MODERN THOUGHT AND NEOLIBERALISM 36

PARADOXAL SUBJECTS 37

RENEWAL OF POLICY 40

SOLIDARITY ECONOMY AS PLACEBO 42

ACKNOWLEDGMENT

To the Counselor of the Spiritist Association of Umbanda São Miguel [Associação Espírita de Umbanda São Miguel], Mr. Miguel Ferreira Neto - also holy father of the Spiritist Center of Umbanda São Miguel [Centro Espírita de Umbanda São Miguel; For the support and logistical support for the writing and publication of this book.

INTRODUCTION

This book is aimed at the common reader minimally acclimated with the Critique of Political Economy of the German philosopher Karl Marx.

The book is an interview with the German philosopher and historian Robert Kurz. Graziela Wolfart and Patricia Fachin conducted the interview.

The interview was held in a year that still felt very close to the heat of the world crisis started with the bursting of the "financial bubble" in October 2008. Because it brought to light: the lack of real accumulation. Nevertheless, a new crisis Keynesianism only shifted the problem of the financial market again to public credit in 2011. Nevertheless, this is at a higher level than in the 1970s. The state has so little competence today, as it had hitherto Long-term accumulation. The crisis of financial markets is replaced by the crisis of public finances.

The German philosopher starts from the observation that the current global crisis is not about a cyclical crisis, from which capitalism will recover later, but it is actually a reflection of the inner economic barrier of capitalism - the internal barrier of valorization of value and the beginning of the ecological external barrier was reached.

Thus, in the author's thesis, defended in his works and in this interview reproduced and annotated here, capitalism has nowhere to expand. For to him, the substance of capital (value) has lost substance. Kurz, anchored in Karl Marx, says that the substance of value is abstract labor. Moreover, this with the microelectronics revolution started in 1980, has lost its aspect of living labor - the abstract work of human wage earners; was and is being continually replaced by the dead labor of the machines. In this way, the value valorization circuit, that is, transformation from abstract to value-added work is not closed.

The world economy, which is increasingly based on an illusion of financially driven growth, is actually involved in the collapse of mortgage credit. Catalyst of a process of devaluation of all financial capital.

Moreover, the apparent exit of appeal to the state will not result in anything, because the state cannot stop the devaluation, but only manage it. Alternatively, in the case of Brazil 2016, adopt increasingly restrictive and repressive measures, such as PEC 55.

Thus, the World Crisis, which broke out in 2008. Continues to spread, is simultaneously and simultaneously a political, fiscal, economic, social, institutional, moral, psychological, sexual and civilizational crisis. That is, for Robert Kurz - German representative of an international movement known as Criticism of Value-Dissociation - the current crisis represents, in fact, the very collapse of capitalism, which the movement referred to earlier started in Germany of the 1980s, names specifically from a commodity-producing society or a modern patriarchal commodity-producing system.

Thus, it is good to reiterate to the reader, according to the paradigm adopted in this book: the present crisis presents itself as the final or terminal crisis of capitalism, the crisis of the value-form itself and not only of its secondary aspects.

The following aspects and developments are part of this crisis:

A). an ecological crisis

B. The impossibility, in the epoch of globalization, for politics and for national states, to continue to function as regulatory bodies.

w. The crisis of the subject constituted by value-dissociation, particularly visible in the crisis of the relationship between the sexes.

D. The exhaustion of the labor society and its foundations. For new potentials of rationalization have eliminated industrial labor from the productive process.

And. The exhaustion of the so-called Money Society as a logical and immediate consequence of the desubstantiation of value, in the elimination of the living labor of wage earners in the face of the premise, adopted by the interviewee, that the capacity for rationalization is greater than the capacity for expansion. In this way, a new job creation phase has ceased to exist.

F. A devaluation of money that corresponds to an immediate devaluation of the goods, because in the game of competition each capitalist will try to cheapen his product to become competitive.

For Robert Kurz, modern production faces a deadlock: reducing working time to a minimum or continuing with working time as a measure of production. For the first time in human history, new technology saves more work than is necessary to expand new product markets.

The goal of modern production has been to turn money into more money through labor producing goods. This is because money has become, in capitalism, the visible form of a real abstraction, value, which is the foundation of capitalism. Moreover, this was only possible because, in capitalism, value represents work. Moreover, the valuation of money appears, then, as a form of wealth constituted by the expenditure of direct human labor, based on the working time. At the same time that capitalism for this purpose creates the sphere separate from work, it dissociates all other activities of production, reproduction and care with life, delegating them to women. Herein lies the heart of the capitalist system, the production of value, the valuation of money.

However, to make a profit, the sale of the goods produced must yield more money than the cost of its production. It achieves this goal the company that makes cheaper offers of goods. In the face of competition, who decides is productivity? In order to produce large quantities of products with low living expenses, that is, few workers and many cheap goods, it becomes indispensable to use machines more and more. Therefore, reducing costs requires fewer workers to produce more products.

Despite this contradiction, the system expanded. In addition, it expanded, because the capacity for rationalization was, now, smaller than the expansion of the market. As a result, the industry absorbed old branches of artisanal production, created new productive sectors, invented new products never imagined and infused the thirst of buying from consumers. The process of increasing productivity, expansion and saturation of markets, creation of new needs and new expansion seemed to have no limit.

However, in the 1980s, the third industrial revolution, based on microelectronics, led the Fordist industries to reach their saturation history. New and sophisticated products have had their prices cheap. Nevertheless, this new economic outbreak did not bring the corresponding increase of jobs. Production has come to depend less on working time and on the amount of labor employed and more on the sophisticated machines in production, created by science and technology.

Faced with the immense accumulation of dead labor, the living labor reduced to mere supervision and maintenance of the mechanical system. The unceasing increase in labor productivity has reached a situation where the new value added per unit of output is insignificant and stingy. As a result, measurement by the criterion of value has become unsustainable. Thus, neither work nor working time are more the main conditions of production. Work begins to cease to be the main source of wealth and work time ceases to be its measure. Here begins the extermination of the golden egg hen of capital, labor.

Today a rupture in our time, at the beginning of the 21st century, demands an even deeper and radical transformation both theoretical and practical. The new productive forces of microelectronics are responsible for the new crisis of capitalism. The material wealth now produced is the result of a sophisticated technological complex. The expenditure of abstract human labor has lost its race to science. Before, Fordism marked the apogee of the system, now, computerization marks its final entry into crisis. This central aspect explains the cause and nature of the current crisis in the globalized world. This is not a particular aspect, but a determining factor in the collapse of modernization. The material content of production has become incompatible with form imposed by value.

This book is based on the formulations of the international Critical Dissociation Category Criticism movement. This movement starts from the premise of repulse the basic ontological classifications of capitalism (labor, value, dissociation, commodity, money, market, state, nation, politics, democracy, fetishism, subject, etc.). In addition, he sees in this list of categories the very irrational character of the modern patriarchal commodity-producing system.

The book draws on the formulations of the German philosopher, historian, pedagogue and publicist Robert Kurz, German representative of the Categorical Critique of Value-Dissociation Movement.

The author, Charles Odevan Xavier, graduated in Portuguese and his respective Literature from the Federal University of Ceará, studied 14 credits of the Master's Degree in Brazilian Literature from the Federal University of Ceará and currently holds a bachelor's degree in Social Sciences from the Federal University of Ceará.

Its connection with the subject is given more on the side of political action than properly for exhibiting some diploma in the area of Economics. Despite this lack of curriculum, the author has the habit of consulting academic journals on the subject, which follow the international parameters of the best universities in the world. As can be seen in the rigor of the bibliography shown at the end of the work.

The author acknowledges his debt of gratitude to the researcher and essayist Jorge Paiva, from whom he absorbed deep insights into the sometimes-arid core of Karl Marx's critique of political economy. Like its indebtedness to the other members of the group of Radical Criticism, a group of dissident activists who dialogue with the theses of the international movement of the Categorical Critique of Value-Dissociation.

KARL MARX: LIVE OR DEAD?

IHU On-Line - In what sense are Marx's theories important for understanding? The current crisis moment in the global financial system?

Robert Kurz - The importance of Marx's critique of political economy in explaining the present great financial crisis is first apparent at two levels: on the one hand, a fundamental aspect is its derivation of the monetary form in the first volume of Capital, on the other, in its credit analysis, mainly in the third volume. In these questions, here, I can only deal with a few elementary points. The classical and neoclassical bourgeois economy starts counterfactually with a pure economy of goods and natural relations of exchange between the subjects of the market. She abstracts from money and speaks of the "veil of money" over "proper" economic transactions. Money, there, appears as a mere sign, without its own content, as a legal construct based on a social convention or a governmental decree. For the economy to work, it is only necessary to adjust the quantity of money to the quantity of goods (quantity theory). For Marx, on the other hand, money is not the secondary "veil", but the premise and central vehicle, an end in itself, of the capitalist valorization (Verwertung).

It is the general presentation of the value embodied in the goods, that is, the value.

Aggregate, which must once again become the monetary form, which, in turn, already represents its starting point. Therefore, money cannot be a mere sign. However, must itself have the character of a commodity, including the "king" of commodities. Money is "generic commodity" set aside, or "generic equivalent," whose "utility value" does not consist in its concrete utility, but in its property of representing the abstract value or aggregate value of the whole commodity world. For everyday transactions, it is true that monetary signs can take the place of commodity money itself, but ultimately, and especially in crises, the real value content of money needs to be redeemed as "royal commodity." Therefore, for Marx, money cannot be totally emancipated from noble metals as monetary commodity, not because of the natural metallic character, but because of the social value represented there in a "concentrated" way.

THE ISSUE OF CREDIT AND INTEREST

Credit comes from the subdivision of capital into production capital or commodity capital, on the one hand, and monetary or capital-interest-yielding capital, on the other. The doubling of the commodity in "vulgar merchandise" (gemeiner Warenpöpel) and money as "royal commodity" is repeated at the level of capital. In bourgeois economics, there is no systematic connection between monetary theory and credit theory. The notion of money as "veil" and mere sign is in contradiction with the notion of moneymaking money as a sort of sui generis production of commodities. Roughly, they assume that the "financial industry" would be as real commodity production as, for example, the automotive industry. Interest seems an independent form of benefit. Marx, on the other hand, shows the illusory character of this notion. It proves that credit, or capital that generates profits, is only a derived form, without proper formation of value. Interest is the price of the capitalist function of credit, a price that must be subtracted from the aggregate social value of real commodity production. In bourgeois statistics, on the other hand, the "products" of money capital added to the social product, thereby distorting the real picture of values.

THE ISSUE OF CREDIT AND INTEREST

Credit comes from the subdivision of capital into production capital or commodity capital, on the one hand, and monetary or capital-interest-yielding capital, on the other. The doubling of the commodity in "vulgar merchandise" (gemeiner Warenpöpel) and money as "royal commodity" is repeated at the level of capital. In bourgeois economics, there is no systematic connection between monetary theory and credit theory. The notion of money as "veil" and mere sign is in contradiction with the notion of moneymaking money as a sort of sui generis production of commodities. Roughly, they assume that the "financial industry" would be as real commodity production as, for example, the automotive industry. Interest seems an independent form of benefit. Marx, on the other hand, shows the illusory character of this notion. It proves that credit, or capital that generates profits, is only a derived form, without proper formation of value. Interest is the price of the capitalist function of credit, a price that must be subtracted from the aggregate social value of real commodity production. In bourgeois statistics, on the other hand, the "products" of money capital are added to the social product, thereby distorting the real picture of values.

MONEY VERSUS DOLLAR

In the twentieth century, money and the entire monetary system were definitively emancipated from gold as real money commodities. In appearance, the last move of this emancipation was the abandonment of dollar convertibility into gold in 1973. This correlates with the fact that, in the subsequent period, money capital also increasingly decoupled from real commodity production. The inflated credit generated not only formidable mountains of debt, which always had to be "rolled", but acquired a form of circulation independent of financial securities (stocks, mortgage bonds, derivatives), where fictitious values of astronomical dimensions were created. In the positivist view, it was simply "facts" that seemed to be based on themselves. Even left-wing theorists, explicitly or implicitly, abandoned the Marxist theory of money and credit, because in appearance it was empirically refuted.

THE CONTRADICTION EXPLAINING THE CRISIS

This 35-year period since the end of the convertibility of the dollar into gold, which is a brief historical period, has now closed in 2008. The true character of this process is now shown. In a secular process, capital, due to rising preliminary costs of production based on scientific technology, became increasingly dependent on credit as anticipation of real future benefit. The growing and over-inflated financial bubbles in recent decades have finally smashed the connection between "fictitious capital" and real value-added production; the anticipation of future value added can never be redeemed. This contradiction has matured and is being discharged as a global financial crisis. This destroys not only the illusion of growth "touched by finance" but also the illusion of money as a mere sign. It goes through dramatic appreciation against all currencies. Nevertheless, the remonetalization of gold is not possible, because the powers of production historically achieved can no longer be represented as "abstract wealth" (Marx) in the form of added value. The devaluation of money corresponds to the devaluation of the mass of goods. In other words, material resources, scientific-technological aggregates, human capabilities and needs can no longer be compressed into the basic forms of capital. On the other hand, as Marx put it in the "fundamentals": "the value-based mode of production collapses"; the "value devaluation" is manifested as the historical limit of the capital appreciation [Verwertung].

THE STATE AS A LAST CREDITOR

In this situation, the state appears as lender of last resort. For bourgeois theory, the state is not the other side, the political side of the capital relationship, but an "extra-economic instance." Also on the left, the illusion of the state has a long tradition. Marx no longer came to conclude the formulation of his theory of the state. Nevertheless, already in the writings of his early stage, he criticized the state-political illusion as a "false public cause." In his theory of credit, in the third volume of Capital, state credit is defined as a special form of fictitious capital, which remains dependent on the real appreciation of capital. In fact, the vexation of state illusion is not today, an illusion that was on the rise after the great crisis in the first half of the twentieth century. In the West, Keynesian state regulation and the growth induced by the expansion of state credit in the early 1980s failed because of boundless inflation. In the East, Soviet state capitalism of the "redemption of modernization" in the late 1980s was defaulted and collapsed. These were already forms in which the historic "value devaluation" was presented. At the neoliberal turn, state intervention, supposedly "extra-economic", was blamed for the dilemma and replaced by a market radicalism. This turn, however, did not overcome the internal barrier of appreciation, but through a policy of deregulation and monetary flooding by central banks, it only opened the floodgates for an expansion of private credit and the bubble-based economy as never before.

THE STATE: AGAIN THE SAVIOR?

After this illusion has also erupted and the market has failed grandiose, it is suddenly intended that the state be the savior again. However, the problem can no longer be solved with further monetary flooding by the state central banks, through a conventional reduction of the interest rate. It turns out that this type of monetary flood always still presupposes the fiction of a "cover" by real processes of valorization, which has already become illusory.

Commercial banks are still only able to deposit "guarantees" with central banks that have ceased to be so, because they consist largely of bad debts. This prevents new financial bubbles from infiltrating in the conventional way. The collapse of mortgage credit was only the catalyst for a process of devaluation of all financial capital, which goes much further. So now, the crisis is raised to the level of the "last instance", that is, of the public finances themselves.

Nevertheless, the state is not a demiurge independent of the laws of capital appreciation. In the past fiscal year, the US public debt tripled even before the recent dramatic crisis; and, if state guarantees are invoked around the world, the result can only be a major public finance crisis. The State cannot stop the devaluation, but only manage it. On the other hand, in the form of deflation, if you put a limit on your own indebtedness, or in the form of inflation, if you print out bills without any "cover". In this new situation in history, even deflationary and inflationary processes may occur in parallel.

IHU On-Line - What in the present crisis represents the Marxist theory of abstract labor as the substance of capital?

Robert Kurz - The classical bourgeois economy was also based on a theory of the "value of labor". Value should ultimately be determined by human labor. It turns out that this theory of the "value of labor" was uncritical and incoherent. The Marxist theory of the determination of value and value added through abstract labor is fundamentally different. The concept of abstract labor is understood critically and strictly negatively as "real abstraction" of the concrete production of goods. In the process of production and circulation of capital, productive activity is reduced, in its social form, to the abstract expenditure of human energy or the application of abstract labor as "expenditure [Verausgabung] of nerve, muscle, brain "(Marx). Where the concrete content of this expenditure is totally indifferent. The mass of abstract labor, once realized, presents itself as a mass of social value and as "objective value" [Wertgegenständlichkeit] of the products. In "value valorization", what matters is not the mass of value itself, but only the mass of value added, which is distributed to the different capitals by the competition mechanism. Valuation as an end in itself also transforms into itself the abstract work that gives rise to it, a work that forms the substance of capital as the expenditure of abstract human energy.

OF THE VALUE FOR THE FUNCTIONAL RELATIONSHIP

Bourgeois neoclassicism abandoned the classical theory of "work value." The value was reduced to the price, being understood no more like common substance of the goods, but like mere function in the interrelationship of the goods. In addition, bourgeois philosophy shifted from "concept of substance" to "concept of function". It was intended to eliminate the problem of the substance, transforming it into an empty functional relation. The "mathematization" of neoclassical "models" is based on this transformation of value into a strictly functional relationship. With this, the theory of value was adapted to the theory of money as a mere "sign". In a sense, this functional "circulatory theory" of value in the German language also succeeded in entering into a so-called "rereading of Marx," where the Marxist critical theory of "labor value" was rejected, being "naturalistic" Or "substantialist", denying that money was merchandise. .

THE QUESTION OF THE LABOR

As in bourgeois economics, this excludes, in principle, an absolute inner barrier to valorization. The reduction to a functional relationship makes the value timeless and eternally regenerative, in appearance. Marx, on the other hand, has shown that capitalist development contains elemental self-contradiction. On the one hand, abstract human energy forms the real substance of capital; On the other hand, competition forms the constant development of productive capacity, which renders human labor superfluous and undermines the substance of value. Until the second industrial revolution of Fordism, this secular process of devaluation of commodities could be compensated for by the mechanism of "relative aggregate value" analyzed by Marx: by the development of productive capacity, the value of "labor" [Arbeitskraft] falls on the social scale and the relative share of value added in the total mass of value increases. This increased relative share of value-added, however, is related to the number of productively usable "labor" [Arbeits kräfte - workers, employees]. Marx did not conclude his theory of the crisis, but implicitly he inferred that the development of productive capacity reaches a point where the number of productively usable "hands" is reduced to the point that the mass of added value Absolute falls. So even the relative increase in value added per manpower is useless. This point is reached with the third industrial revolution of microelectronics. The historical relative value-added compensation mechanism is extinguished, the absolute real value-added mass falls, and the "value devaluation" leads to the desubstantiation of capital.

CAPITALISM REDUCED TO ITS REAL CONDITIONS OF VALORIZATION

This is the reason why, in the previous period, more valuation could be simulated only through financial bubbles devoid of substance. When these burst, however, no new "zero point" is reached, from which real appreciation can begin again. Instead, capitalism is reduced to its real conditions of valorization, whose pattern of productive capacity is irreversible. This substantial theory of the crisis, which speaks of an absolute lower barrier of capital, has often been criticized as "technological" by the left. Nevertheless, this is not the technical aspect, but the effect of technology on the conditions of recovery. Marx did not formulate a functional theory of value in "timeless" terms, but rather the theory of a historical and dynamic development of capital as the displacement of real substance, conveyed by the increasing application of scientific and technological potentials, and which cannot be infinitely prolonged.

THE TENSION IN THE ADMINISTRATION OF THE CRISIS

On this point, two observations must be made. In the first place, Marx's categories are real categories of a logic of society as a whole, which is based on empirical phenomena, but cannot be described directly empirically. This is because empirically capital does not only shift in complex and contradictory placements, but the real aggregation of the substance of social value always only presents itself in retrospect. Bourgeois statistics never capture the real mass of value or aggregate value, but only the superficial flows of commodity and money, which produce a distorted image. Therefore, the crashes are also not predicted, but present themselves in an eruptive way, when the basal logic erupts into empiricism, as it seems to be the case today. Chaotic curves and uncontrolled jumps, for example, of the exchange rate or stock market indices necessarily have to be attributed to the non-empirical nature of capital and its substantial evolution. This is not within the reach of a permanent or affirmative categorical theory, which can only run after unpredictable phenomena. In addition, the valuation barrier is strictly objective. What "falls" through the curves is the ability of capital to reproduce itself socially. Nevertheless, what does not fall by itself are the forms of consciousness or "objective forms of thought" constituted by capital (Marx). By reaching the historical limit of capitalism, a colossal tension arises between the impossibility of continuing a real valorization and a generalized mentality that has internalized the capitalist conditions of existence and does not want nor can imagine anything other than living within these forms. The difficult task is to resolve this tension in the process of resistance against crisis management, or capitalism will lead to a world catastrophe. For this, a left is not prepared that has adjusted more and more to capitalist development.

IHU On-Line - What are the consequences of the financial crisis for the worldwide level of employment?

Robert Kurz Since the beginning of the third industrial revolution in the 1980s, the new potentials of rationalization have eliminated industrial labor from the production process on a scale never seen before. Consequently, cycle-by-cycle increased unemployment and under-employment on a global scale. The reverse of the medal was the simulation of valorization by the influx of "fictitious capital". Unlike earlier epochs of capitalism, however, there was no rapid devaluation of money-deprived money capital to give way to new real accumulation. Instead, because of the lack of new possibilities for real appreciation, an unprecedented historical interweaving of economies based on the financial bubble and the conjuncture began. The "fictitious values" were not restricted to the Financial Eden, but for a long time and to an increasing extent they were transferred to the apparent real economy. Thus, the famous growth "touched by finances" appeared, which seemed to discourage the economic laws of capitalism and allowed a wave of deficit difficulties, which in reality had no solid foundation. Although mass unemployment increased, it was held in relative limits because, in the midst of deficit situations, "fictitious jobs" were created, which financial bubbles devoid of substance fueled.

THE DISTINCTION BETWEEN "PRODUCTIVE WORK" AND "IMPRODUCTIVE WORK"

To understand this evolution, it is important to distinguish Marx between "productive work" and "unproductive". All activities in the formal capitalist context are abstract labor, which is represented in money. Nevertheless, not all-abstract work is productive in capitalist terms, nor does it contribute to the mass of real social value added. Certain functions of the capital relation are in themselves unproductive and with "dead costs."

In addition, industrial productive activity can become unproductive in the capitalist sense, when it exceeds the capacity

[Fassungsvermögen] of real value-added production ("idle capacities"). All the results of abstract work take the form of merchandise as "circulation objectivity." When they get a price, they take on a share of the mass of social value added, failing that if their output contributed to that mass. This global social character [gesamtgesellschaftlich] of the production of value and value-added is not very clear in Marx. This is the reason why the famous problem of value-price transformation arose. However, this problem is solved when the mass of social value added is not based on a sum of "individual" commodity values, but represents a substantial, global, non-quantifiable mass in terms of business administration; its quantity is revealed only by competition at the circulation level. This does not make the problem of substance irrelevant, but it has nothing to do with a substance of value of the individual commodity.

AN IMPROPER OCCUPATION

What does this mean for the era of economics based on the financial bubble? The fall in the mass of real social value added was masked, in appearance, by the "fictitious aggregate value" of the inflated credit system. In this way, an unproductive occupation was generated that far surpassed the capacity [Fassungsvermögen] of the real production of added value. First, along with the "financial industry", employment in this sector has swelled disproportionately, a job that produces no value, only intermedia financial transactions. In addition, an equally disproportionate sector of personal services unproductive in capitalist terms has been created: from the advertising industry, the information industry and the media, the sports industry and culture. Precisely in these sectors, the depletion of substance was implemented, on the one hand, as an astronomically excessive remuneration of small elite of stars and, on the other hand, as precarization in the form of freelancers, pseudo-autonomous and entrepreneurs of misery. Third, the global deficit situation forced the occupation of an "aristocracy of workers" in the export industries (automotive production, machinery), which was also unproductive because it was based not on real value-added profits and wages, but was fueled by financial bubbles.

THE ABSTRACT WORK SYSTEM LEADS TO THE ABSURD TO SELF

To the extent that the bursting of the financial bubbles reduces capitalism to its real conditions of appreciation, much of the unproductive employment will also have to fall. The real mass of value-added is too small to describe the "objectivity of circulation" of these inflated sectors as "value objectivity." The global depression to be expected will not only lead to a large part of the capitalist financiers "owners of the universe" but also a large part of those who depend on them: poor service providers, freelancers, low wage earners, temporary workers, as well as jobs in the export. The system of abstract labor leads to the absurd itself; and minority global capitalism suffers its Waterloo, even though no one wants to take notice, although everyone knows it intuitively.

IHU On-Line - What is the weight of capitalism in today's society, characterized by virtual relationships, immaterial work and autonomy?

Robert Kurz - The concepts cited come from the postmodern ideology, which from the beginning accompanied and formulated neoliberal financial capitalism of the "fictitious capital" inflated. Already in the late 1970s, in his book The Symbolic Exchange and Death (São Paulo: Loyola, 1996), Baudrillard explained the relationship with the economy by establishing "fictitious capital" as a new principle of reality. In addition, Derrida, in a text about "false money", affirmed the virtuality of capital. The postmodern radical rejection of "essentialism" or "substantialism" corresponds to capital's attempt to slyly circumvent its own "Aristotelian" problem of substance. The cult of "virtuality" permeated all occupations, even personal relationships. The reduction of value to a functional relation led to the paradoxical "absolutization of relativity", which, in the ordinary understanding, was reflected as "arbitrariness". Economic virtualism corresponded to the technological virtualism of the internet, which underwent a mutation into the second life of individualized abstract existences of bloggers, who are unable to organize and resist in real terms.

AND LEFT?

The postmodern left was an orphan in this process. Which reduced the social struggle to virtual and symbolic level. Antônio Negri's "post-operaticism" expresses this ideology. The objective fetishism of capital is denied and, together with the crisis, reduced to subjective relations of will. The place of the radical critique of abstract labor and the [abstract] form of value is taken by the illusion of an "autonomous self-valuation" of freelancers of "immaterial labor." This concept does not make sense, because all abstract work, even if it does not lead to material products, is "worn out by nerve, muscle, brain." Nevertheless, unproductive 'cognitive work', in capitalist terms, does nothing to contribute to the real mass of social added value. The "autonomy" of this particular form of abstract labor is illusory, because it remains dependent on the world market. It is the illusion of a new middle class that has lost its foundation. When capitalism is brought back to its real conditions of valorization, the "self-valorization" of abstract labor in the sectors of "knowledge" and media communication is also extinguished. The vexation of the financial bubble economy is also the vexation of the postmodern left and its ideological "anti-substantiality," which claims to declare every manifestation of life as "valorization." The basis of this illusion is not economic, but "existentialist," for it resorts to Heidegger. By bursting the financial bubble economy, the postmodern "heideggerization" of the left runs the risk of leading to nationalist and anti-Semitic sentiments.

THE LEFT AND THE SUBJECT-OBJECT DIALECTICS OF MODERN FETISH

IHU On-Line - Are the current financial and ecological crises related to the collapse of modernization?

Robert Kurz - The term collapse is a provocative buzzword, generally used in a pejorative sense, in order to disqualify the representatives of a radical theory of the crisis as "apocalyptic", not to be taken seriously. Not only the capitalist elites, but also the representatives of the left prefer to believe that capitalism can be renewed forever. Of course, a global social system does not collapse overnight as an infarcted individual. However, the era of capitalism has passed. After all, modernization was nothing more than the implementation and development of this system, which was not the case if the mechanisms were private capitalism or state capitalism. In spite of all external differences, the common ground consists in the "valorization of value", that is, in the transformation from "abstract labor" to "added value". However, this is not a subjective purpose, but an end in itself that ended up becoming independent. Both capitalists and wage earners, as well as state agents, are nothing more than officials of this end in and of themselves who have been uncontrollable, which Marx called the "automatic subject." In this case, universal competition forces a blind dynamics of the development of productive capacity, which constantly generates new conditions of valorization to finally find an absolute historical barrier. The inner economic barrier consists in the fact that the development of the productive force leads to a point where "abstract labor" as a "substance" of "aggregate value" is so reduced by rationalization of the productive process that it is impossible to increase the real value [Reale Verwertung]. The "decapitalalization of capital" or "devaluation of value" means that the products themselves are no longer commodities, but can be represented in monetary form as a generic form of value, and are merely consumer goods. The purpose of capitalist production, however, is not the manufacture of consumer goods to satisfy needs, but the end in itself, which is valorization. Therefore, according to capitalist criteria, when the internal economic barrier is reached, it is necessary to close production and, therefore, the vital process of society, even if all means are available.

VIRTUAL CAPITALISM

In real terms, this situation had already arisen in the mid-1980s, with the third industrial revolution. Capitalism has prolonged its life in a "virtualized" form, on the one hand, through historically unprecedented indebtedness (anticipation of future added value, which in reality can never be redeemed); On the other hand, by the swelling, never seen before, of the so-called financial bubbles (stocks and real estate). This pseudo accumulation of "devoid of substance" money capital was also used to feed the actual production of commodities. This resulted in a global deficit in terms of single-export flows, mainly to the United States. The export processing zones of China and India, however, do not represent a real expansion of "abstract labor" because its starting point was not real purchasing power, but the "devoid of substance" money capital represented in the indebtedness And financial bubbles. For more than two decades, he had harbored the illusion that "growth touched exclusively by finance" would be viable. By no means, the end of this illusion consists exclusively in a financial crisis. The decanted "real economy," in fact, has long since become more real, having been artificially fed with "no-substance" financial bubbles. Now capitalism is reduced to its real foundations of valorization. The consequence is a new crisis in the world economy, with no new potential for real appreciation. At the same time, capitalism comes up against its natural external limitation. So much so, that "abstract labor" became superfluous as a transformation of human energy into "added value." The expansion of the technological application of fossil fuels (oil, gas) has accelerated. The blind dynamics of the development of uncontrolled productive capacity led, on the one hand, to the predictable depletion of fossil energy resources and, on the other, to the destruction of the global climate and the natural environment, to an equally predictable degree. The external natural barrier and the inner economic barrier have diverse time horizons. While the end of the real "valorization of value" is already in the past and the capitalist economy is going through its historical crisis now, in the space of a few years (roughly over the next decade), the absolute natural barrier is still in the (Within a maximum period of two to three decades). The economic crisis and the concomitant closure of production capacities restrain the depletion of energy resources at the expense of growing global social misery in the capitalist form. At the same time, however, the processes of destruction of the natural bases and the climate are so advanced that they cannot be stopped by the economic crisis, and the external natural barrier will be reached despite everything.

CAPITALIST DESTRUCTION OF NATURE

The end of modernization means, therefore, that, in addition to having to overcome the capitalist form of reproduction, a post-capitalist world society will have to suffer and deal with the consequences of the capitalist destruction of nature for a long time. For the analysis and theoretical critique of the crisis, it is important to see the internal interconnection of the two historical barriers of capitalism. There is, however, the danger of throwing against each other these two aspects of the historical crisis; this applies to both sides: for the capitalist elites as well as for the representatives of an "ecological reductionism", which only admits the external natural barrier. Capitalist crisis management and ecological reductionism could enter into a perverse alliance, which would deny the economic barrier and, in the name of the ecological crisis, preach to the depleted and miserable masses an ideology of "social renunciation." Against this, it must be maintained that the crisis, the criticism and the overcoming of the capitalist structure take precedence, because the destruction of nature is a consequence, and does not cause the internal barrier of that system.

IHU On-Line - Why do you say that the vexation of the crisis is also the vexation of the postmodern left?

Robert Kurz - The crisis is no shame, but an objective process, resulting from the blind dynamics of competition and uncontrolled development of production capacity. As far as the postmodern left is concerned, one can speak of vexation insofar as it discards, for the most part, the critique of political economy. The "economism" of traditional party Marxists has only been criticized for eliminating the negative objectivity of the capitalist categories from "abstract labor" and "valorization of value". The crisis dynamics inherent in capitalism went completely unnoticed, having been translated into "unlimited possibilities". Like the neoliberal elites. The postmodern left believed in "growth touched by finance" and became the ideological expression of fictitious capital. Economic virtualism was complemented by the technological virtualism of the internet. Second Life of virtual space underwent the mutation of becoming the "proper" way of life and Antônio Negri's supposed "immaterial work" ended up being the continuation of the capitalist ontology of work. The real substance problem of "abstract labor" was denied; an "anti-socialist" ideological (or "anti-essentialism") to contrast. Marx denounced this problem of substance as a mere metaphysics of outmoded thinking, rather than recognizing it as a "real metaphysics" of capitalism, which is still quite material. At the same time an orientation through the circulation sphere occurred. The capitalist financial illusion, from which acts of buying and selling could also generate growth, such as the actual production of commodities, was also the implicit premise of postmodern thought. The indebted subject of the market and consumption appeared as the bearer of reproduction and of a possible emancipation, and no more could be said in what it would consist. False economic and technological virtualism had its philosophical counterpart in an epistemology that no longer wanted to criticize and overcome the fetishistic "real appearance" of the capital relation, but it lured to the belief that one could "realize oneself" under those conditions. Following the virtualistic illusions, the "iron cage" (Max Weber) of the commodity-producing system was redefined as "ambivalence" and "contingency" open to everything and at any time. Even the negative truth of criticism would have no more objective basis under prevailing conditions, but could be "produced" and "negotiated." To the postmodern left, the negative nature of capital dissolved into an indefinable "plurality" of phenomena, which would be presented as disconnected "plurality" of social movements, without focusing on the concrete core of the capital.

POST-MODERN THOUGHT AND NEOLIBERALISM

In social terms, the postmodern left was a trendsetter of capitalist individualization and flexibilization. The abstract flexi-individual was not recognized as a form of the bourgeois subject in crisis, but it received the nimbo of anticipation of the liberated individuality already in the bosom of capitalism. Instead of appearing as the ultimate form of the totalitarian market's existence and as a threatening "war of all against all" in the universal competition of the crisis. Individualization appeared as an atomized form of "self-realization" and "flexible human being" (Richard Sennet) presented himself not as a defenseless object to the taste of capitalist impositions, but as his own "sovereign", who could conquer new spaces and transform himself in what he wanted. The proximity of postmodern thinking to neoliberal ideology has always been unquestionable, despite external contrasts. Now the postmodern left is faced with the wreckage of its illusions and is confronted with the harsh reality of a monumental crisis, which from the beginning it did not want to admit and for which it, therefore, is not prepared.

IHU On-Line - Does the left of today live an existential crisis? Before suggesting alternatives to the current crises, would the world left have to solve its own impasses? For you, is there currently a theoretical void left or a "methodological mismatch" in the search for common ground for a theory?

Robert Kurz - The existential crisis of the left today consists precisely in the fact that it has failed to transform Marxism and reformulate the critique of political economy within the standards of the 21st century. For of course there is no return to the paradigms of a bygone age. The label of "post-modernity" was fake, because the real social transformation of capitalism did not inaugurate new social spaces, but it marked the transition to its historical ruin. Neither the end of the old labor movement nor the sinking of "real socialism" was digested critically. The postmodern transition did not overcome traditional Marxism, it only gave continuity to it in an emptied form. As the socialist objective disappeared altogether and the false "plurality" of purely private aspirations dissolved, the paradigm of the "working class" became an unsustainable multitude of false social subjects, In the case of Negri, ended up in the totally empty concept of "multitude", which means everything and nothing. The emptying of the subject has its correlate in a virtualization of the social struggles, which for the most part only have a symbolic character, being less and less capable of real intervention. To characterize this situation with "impasses" of the left is a euphemism. The old left as well as the postmodern left over. There is no more ontological subject of "work", because "work" turned out to be a historical substance of capital and became obsolete. With this, the paradoxical Marxist concept of the "objective subject" itself, which only needs to come "to itself", is settled in historical terms and cannot be continued in substitutes. In this respect, the "theoretical void" of the left is identical with the "methodological mismatch". The Left has never been able to grasp the subject-object dialectic of modern fetishism. The consequence was to fall into a crude objectivism or an equally crude subjectivism. The oscillation between these two poles of fetishism makes up a good part of the left-wing discussions that have not been able to leave behind this polarity.

PARADOXAL SUBJECTS

For a new emancipatory social movement, what matters is no longer to awaken by kissing an "objective subject," but to critique the subject form, without ontological safeguard, and interpret it as a form of capitalist existence. The "subject" form can always only be an agent of the "automatic subject" of the valorization of capital and cannot be confused with the will for emancipatory action, which must itself constitute itself and cannot have an ontological foundation. This is a difficult thing to think about, because the postmodern left just gave up the subject's critique (the late Foucault again appealed to the particularized subject). This criticism failed mainly because it was not connected with the critique of political economy. This problem is also linked to the critique of the modern relationship between genders. It is true that the traditional left and the postmodern left have made their obligatory pretensions to feminism, but never really took its theme seriously. Even feminism itself, in spite of meritorious analyzes, was largely confined to defining women as an "objective subject" as paradoxical as the "working class." The postulate of a female "subject formation", therefore, leads to the same dead end. Feminism was also victimized by the postmodern transition and dissolved the "abgespalten" feminine form of capitalism into a "diversity" of particular emancipatory aspirations that did not touch the central problem. Here again, it would be important to mediate the critique of modern patriarchy with the critique of political economy, not to treat it as a secondary, "derivative," [abgeleitet]. In this case, the notion that the apparently neutral categories of capital and their "subject" form in themselves are already "masculine" is fundamental, and that capitalist "reason" is androcentric in origin. The dissolution of the traditional family and their gender roles does not change the case because the androcentric character of capitalism continues in another way. The critique of these social forms and the critique of the capitalist relationship of genera are mutually dependent and must be thought together. The critique of the "objective subject" of "labor" and "divergent" female existence is not a play on words, but has enormous practical consequences for overcoming capitalism. In this way, too, the notion of the old Marxism of social emancipation and of socialism "within" capitalist categories that would only have to be regulated and moderated in another way was liquidated. At the historical limit of capitalism is the challenge of "categorical criticism", of the connection between "abstract labor", commodity form and "valorization of value" as well as the relation between the sexes in this context. This is also difficult to be thought of, because these existential conditions are internalized, and have been further entrenched by postmodern thought. Only the formulation of a new socialist objective based on a "categorical critique" can lead to the development of immanent transition requirements that are also adequate in the process of historical crisis, thus gaining real power to impose itself. Without the unifying focus on the core of capitalism, social movements remain defenseless and particularized. It is to be feared, however, that the left, caught by surprise by the crisis, end up relying on too narrow conceptions of supposed "salvation", thus only ratifying their historical impotence.

IHU On-Line - In what sense has the current situation contributed to making politics an endangered model. Can we say that the economy "colonized" politics? Are you rethinking politics from what is happening now?

Robert Kurz - State-centered politics as a synthesizing instance of capitalism is moving out of line not because it has been colonized by the economy, but because it has long failed because of its own premises. The problem has not only to do with the external condition of the globalization of capital, which has broken the spaces of national economy. The regulatory force of the state is extinguished mainly by the fact that substantially nothing else has to be regulated. The capitalist valorization in the forms of "abstract labor" of money has always constituted the premise of the state, which it cannot get around. When capital is devalued by its own development of productive capacity, the State can only react to this through inflationary issuance of money by its central bank. This does not overcome the lack of substance of virtualized capital, but exacerbates it as the devaluation of the vehicle-end-in-itself called money. It happens that the competence of the central bank is purely formal; Its generation of money can only give expression to the substantial production of added value through "abstract labor", but it cannot replace it. The limits of state credit had already been reached in the late 1970s. At that time, the expansion of state credit, devoid of substance, was punished by inflationary spikes. The illusion of neoliberalism consisted in attributing inflation exclusively to state activity. Neoliberal deregulation only shifted the problem of state credit to the financial markets. Although the punishment of inflation was delayed because of the transnational character of the financial bubble economy, the inflationary potential began to manifest itself in the global deficit situation until 2008. This process, at first, was interrupted because, since then, capital Virtual world and with it the global situation are giving their last breath. Nevertheless, if now the State is again invoked as "last instance" and deus ex machina, its conjuncture and salvation packages will again have to provoke the devaluation of money itself, only that it will happen at a higher stage of development and in much greater proportion than thirty years ago.

RENEWAL OF POLICY

In this scenario, hope for the "political rebirth" is the greatest of all bubbles. The damage caused by the political limitation of losses will be even greater than the current crisis.

The state can only regulate the definitive death of its capitalism. In this respect, the left is also disoriented as long as it cannot question the very foundations of the system. To the extent that the supposed "autonomy" of the particular and symbolic social movements turns smoke by the inner barrier of valorization, it is to be feared that the left will regress to its traditional statism, because nothing else occurs to it. For the most part, what is meant to be a social criticism of the left is practically nothing more than a little Keynesian nostalgia. If the left hopes to launch its "social reforms" by taking advantage of the tram of the statist administration of the crisis, it will eventually derail along with it and, once it has passed its carnival in virtualism, it will become a trendsetter of inflationary politics. She well desserves this fate.

IHU On-Line - What other leftist forces can arise at this time?

Robert Kurz - If the global left stuck in the capitalist categories fails. You will naturally wonder where there are other forces of social emancipation. Certainly, there will be rebellions and social conflicts when people are deprived of their basic living conditions, however precarious they may be. These eruptions can also take the right path, manifesting as sexism, racism, anti-Semitism and nationalism, although this has no chance of reactionary overcoming the crisis. There are also spontaneous social upheavals that are vaguely understood as leftists, as one can observe in Greece a few months ago. Some leftists, who use them against the necessary theoretical transformation, are already mythicizing these youthful vandals reacting viscerally against the oppression of vital needs. Nevertheless, the cult of spontaneity has always been vexed. The spontaneous revolts of youth, no matter how organized they may be, will not help if they cannot acquire a critical notion of the situation in terms consistent with the times. Therefore, there is no alternative but to develop a new socialist goal through a categorical critique that cannot be linked to the "false immediate character" of spontaneous praxis. It is necessary to put up with this tension so that the emerging social resistance does not die suffocated in its own verbiage to champion "philosophy of life".

IHU On-Line - You say that world society needs to free itself from the game of real economism and organize its resources in a new way, beyond the state and the market. In this sense, how can the left develop revolutionary work and change the current situation? What, in this case, would be the proposals of the left in the face of the international financial crisis?

Robert Kurz - It should be noted that it is precisely society that needs to be liberated globally from the real economics of capital. It is true that a new form of reproduction can only succeed beyond the market and the state. In recent years, this formula has been increasingly used in the sense of being just an alternative, cooperative economy, as it were "side by side" with the social synthesis by capital, and which in some way would gradually expand. This only gives continuity to postmodern "colored" particularism. However, the negative Vergesellschaftung of capitalism can only be completely overcome or not overcome. The cooperative alternative economy has a long history and has always failed, the last time in the 1980s. This crisis of historical proportions does not improve the conditions for such ideas, quite the contrary. This is because an "alternative" reproduction restricted to a small space is not only bound up with unconfessional social impositions, but also depends on the functions of market and state, since on its own it can only meet few vital needs. In addition, the real reproduction of individuals is inserted in a chain that Marx, under capitalist conditions, called "total social work." This structure can only be transformed in its entirety; one cannot start with potatoes or software and think that a "model" has been created on a small scale that only needs to be applied to society as a whole. "Model Platonism" is a product of bourgeois economic theory, not radical criticism. When, in the midst of crisis, due to a lack of "financability": water and electricity are disconnected, when medical assistance and the capitalist distribution of foodstuffs collapse, then what is at stake is not the gradual "networking" of Communes that intend to reform life, or the "network formation" of virtual exchange, but the transformation of the capitalist mode of "network formation" of the whole society. For this, it is necessary the organized resistance of the whole society against the administration of the crisis that stipulates own goals in the level of social synthesis.

SOLIDARITY ECONOMY AS PLACEBO

Hence only the particularistic "solidarity economy" type of placebos, which usually consist of a mix of subsistence economy, illusory "monetary reforms" and abstract communitarian ideology, are diverting attention. He wants to make the Urucubaca a blessing. It is very consistent that these proposals are also dating "solutions to the financial crisis" and are associated with Keynesian nostalgia. There is no longer a solution to the financial crisis; one must attack the very criterion of "financiability" if one is to take seriously a new mode of reproduction that goes beyond the market and the state.

IHU On-Line - Considering that we are in the information age and experiencing the crisis of capital, what new directions will the world of work have in relation to the capital / labor relation? Considering the insertion of new technologies in today's society, but also the current crises. Is it possible to think of deglobalization in the computer age?

Can we think of this as a new world economy?

Robert Kurz - Computer science as the basis of the third industrial revolution just generated the development of the productive capacity that necessarily had to lead to the inner barrier of capitalism. Under capitalist conditions, it is pure "crisis technology", which can only develop positive potentials beyond valuation. The postmodern illusion and financial capitalism consisted in that computing would imply new forms of "immaterial labor" in a so-called information society, as well as new relations between capital and labor, with greater "self-determination" of workers. In fact, the "information age" has in the past led to mass unemployment, underemployment and the precariousness of labor relations. Already the supposed self-determination led to a compulsive "self-accountability" of individuals by the process of valorization. Antônio Negri intended to stylize this negative evolution as an option for an "autonomous self-valuation" (auto valorisazzione). This eventually became a buzzword for the repressive administration of labor, which turned it into a proposal to define individuals as "self-entrepreneurs of their workforce" and as "managers of their own human capital" in order to leave them totally at the mercy of the conditions of capitalism in crisis. The new crisis would dramatically exacerbate these trends and would deny finally attempts to see in the capitalist form of the information society an "ambivalence" with emancipatory potential. The postmodern metaphysics of ambivalence is exhausted. Globalization cannot be reduced to information technology. Under capitalist conditions, it could only be a globalization of capital, under whose command information is also found. It is to be expected that, with the inflationary policy of the State, the processing of the crisis will lead to a "deglobalisation" insofar as the retreat is tested for the protectionist egoism of the national economies, which are still only formal; all accompanied by neo-nationalist ideologies. Only this cannot overcome the crisis if it only aggravates it. One also has to wonder if the internet is sustainable - not because of a possible technological collapse (although there are also indications of capacity depletion) - but because it depends on a formidable infrastructure whose "financiability" is so in doubt as all the rest. A purely virtual globalization is not sustainable if it is not linked to transnational material reproduction beyond capitalism. The maritacas of the blogosphere and the freaks of the internet can still take a fright.

IHU On-Line - How can one speak in ethics in the current mold of capitalist society?

Robert Kurz - In all historical fetishistic formations, ethics has gone from an attempt to socialize with the conditions of reproduction given, presupposed blindly, without overcoming them. Even modern bourgeois ethics seek to resolve contradictions and crises without touching constitutive causes. In it, the place of radical criticism must be assumed by a canon of norms of moral conduct for individuals, so that within existing forms the person may be nice to others. What can fail is not the system, but only the morals of individuals. The current crisis, moreover, has also been attributed to the ethical deficits of bankers and executives. It is not by chance that the highest volume "redemption package" is in ethics, which, for a change, is on the rise. Unfortunately, this package is very hollow. The "automatic subject" is not accessible for any ethical imperatives; Ethics, therefore, is more or less the last thing critical theory should deal with.

GRADES

Value

Both etymologically and in practice, the concept of value seems to designate the "good" as such, the desirable one. Despite the different accentuation, economic value and ethical and cultural "values" are mistaken as synonyms. It is no wonder that the founder of classical political economy, Adam Smith, acted in parallel as a moral philosopher. However, in Marx's inverse conceptualization, economic value is precisely the opposite, the central negative of the commodity society. In it, abstract work, the fetishistic social form of products, is objectified. The expression of a product "having" a so-called value has for it a double meaning. First, while they are economic values, the sensitive quality of the products is extinguished, and they are no longer material representatives of indiscriminate abstract labor, which can only be transformed into the form of incarnation of money. In the second place, however, the social absurdity of the fact that the living process of the appropriation of nature by man and of the social relations which he measures up takes the form of Properties of dead objects. The living activity of men is absorbed, so to speak, by their own products, which by this absurd mechanism are promoted to almost subjects of society, whereas men, their creators, are degraded to mere accessories. In the self-movement of money, this reversal ends. The Marxism of the epigones, in the succession of the bourgeois classics and in contrast to Marx, did not refer in a negative way, but in a positive way to the quality of the products of fetish values, of "good" result of the work, while the concept of objectification was Reduced to a mere phenomenon of consciousness. Criticism focuses exclusively on surplus value, that is, the "unpaid" amount of the productive value, from which the worker is supposed to be deprived. In this way, the destructive quality of socialization in form-value is not criticized, but only the quantitative mechanism of distribution that is found on this blindly presupposed basis.

(In. O Colapso da Modernização - *Da derrocada do socialismo de caserna à crise da economia mundial* de Robert Kurz; Editora Paz e Terra, Brasil, 2ª edição, 1993.)

Monetarism

Common name for a special economic theory, born of the neoclassic national-economic neoliberalism - and is strictly against the state regulation of demand, advocated by Keynesianism. As Adam Smith, the "self-healing forces of the market" and his invisible hand are conjured up, which, nevertheless, would require the support of a strictly anti-inflationary and restrictive monetary policy. Milton Friedman, with his Chicago school, is considered the principal representative. It is almost always understood by monetarism that practical economic policy, a radical market advocate, is linked to this theory and that in the 1980s, with the names of "reaganomics" and "Thatcherism", particularly conquered the United States and Great Britain , Although with very catastrophic results. However, one can also understand by monetarism, in a much more general and fundamental sense, the principle of competition or the coactive operation of the laws of money in general. This principle is opposed, as a reverse of the same medal, statism, and state intervention in the process almost naturally arising from competition, in order to change its course or prevent its consequences. As political-economic ideologies, monetarism and statism struggle for political-social hegemony, they also interpenetrate constantly and refer to the same basic structure objectified as abstract labor, that is, the self-valorization of money. Therefore, in statist epochs of the commodity-production system the monetarist element always acts, and vice versa, distinguishing themselves only by the accentuation.

Fordism

Modern sociological designation for the most recent development phase of modern commodity production, stretching from about 1920 to 1980. Denomination named after Henry Ford, who invented the treadmill in automobile assembly. With this, the last remnants of craftsmanship could be eliminated from the industrial work process. The "engineer-business fundamentals" of the American engineer Taylor, that is, the decomposition of production processes and their synthetic recomposition, under the command of the economic logic of "optimal" entanglement, could only be realized on a large scale by virtue of Of production on the Ford crawler. Thus, it became possible, far beyond the automobile industry, the mass production in many sectors that until then escaped the calculation of valuation of business administration. It was only after World War II that Fordism was universally imposed. The new mass-production industries not only became the center of unparalleled capital accumulation, but also of a "social model," of a way of living, marked by the aggregation of abstract labor in combination with a "Free time ". Since the early 1980s, Fordism has been running out in every respect; Ecological crises, mass industrial unemployment, outsourcing ("service society"), new forms of depletion and system collapse in much of the world have provoked numerous criticisms of the Fordist way of living.

BIBLIOGRAPHY

Emancipe-se: Anteprojeto Crítica Radical – Fortaleza: Crítica Radical, 2016.

JAPPE, Anselm. **As aventuras da mercadoria: para uma nova crítica do valor** – [tradução: José Miranda Justo] – Lisboa: Antígona, 2006.

KURZ, Robert. **O Colapso da Modernização - Da derrocada do socialismo de caserna à crise da economia mundial** - Editora Paz e Terra, Brasil, 2ª edição, 1993.

KURZ, Robert. **Razão Sangrenta. Ensaios sobre a crítica emancipatória da modernidade capitalista e seus valores ocidentais** – [tradução de Fernando R. De Moraes Barros] - São Paulo: Hedra, 2010.

OUTHWAITE, William; BOTTOMORE, Tom. **Dicionário do pensamento social do Século XX** – [Com a consultoria de Ernest Gellner, Robert Nisbet, Alain Touraine; - Editoria da versão brasileira: Renato Lessa, Wanderley Guilherme dos Santos - Tradução de Eduardo Francisco Alves, Álvaro Cabral. — Rio de Janeiro: Jorge Zahar Ed., 1996

Projeto Alternativo: a saída pra vida plena de sentido/Movimento Sair do Capitalismo; Grupo Crítica Radical; colaboração de Robert Kurz; Roswitha Scholz; Anselm Jappe, Fortaleza: Sem Fronteiras, 2012.

SCHOLZ, Roswitha. **O valor é o homem: teses sobre a socialização pelo valor e a relação entre os sexos** – [tradução: José Marcos Macedo] – *In: NOVOS ESTUDOS-CEBRAP, Nº. 45-São Paulo, Julho de 1996, PP. 15-36*

Wolfart, Graziela; Fachin, Patricia. **O vexame da economia da bolha financeira é também o vexame da esquerda pós-moderna** – In: *CADERNOS IHU EM FORMAÇÃO ANO 5 Nº 34 2009.*

www.ingramcontent.com/pod-product-compliance
Lightning Source LLC
Chambersburg PA
CBHW021445170526
45164CB00001B/397